THIS BOOK BELONGS TO

____

Made in United States
Orlando, FL
02 November 2023

38513621R00057